DATES IN THE STATES

A COUPLE TRAVELING THE UNITED STATES ON A BUDGET

Mystery Date
Nashville, TN

By Dates in the States

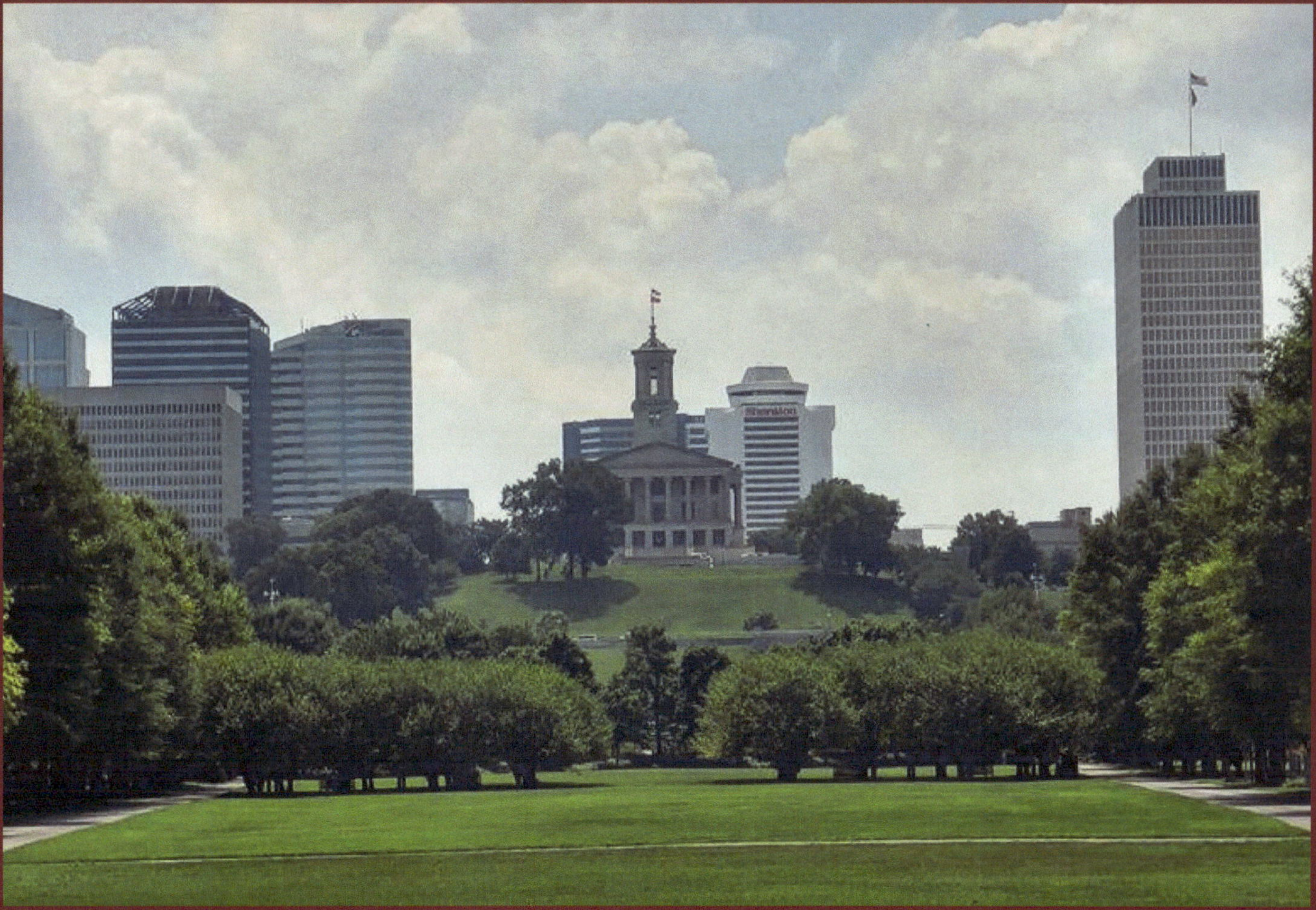

"Our passion is travel, and we want to share our adventures to inspire others to explore the world with their loved ones. Dare to live beyond the box."

Dates in the States

Introduction

Hey there! We're Crystal and Shane, the duo behind Dates in the States, where we share our love for discovering unique adventures, unforgettable moments, and hidden gems across the U.S. Whether you're searching for a fun date idea, a new place to explore, or just a little inspiration, we've got you covered!

Our Mystery Date Books are designed to help people shake up their routine and experience the best local spots in a fun, intentional way. Inside, you'll find a curated collection of date ideas. Each one meant to be completed over the course of a single day in a specific neighborhood. All of which are a surprise until you flip the page!

Think of it as a playful challenge to try something new, support local businesses, and see your city through a different lens. Our hope is that this book helps you explore more, laugh more, and feel more connected, not just to the people you're with, but to the place you're visiting or call home.

Here's What To Expect:

In this Mystery Date Book, we're taking you to the North side of Nashville, TN where iconic landmarks, rich music history, and some of the city's most beloved food spots come together for a full day of exploring.

Here's what to expect for your day ahead:

Start your morning with a classic breakfast at an old soda shop. From there, stretch your legs and soak up local history as you wander through open green space and one of Nashville's most vibrant gathering spots. Midday brings a deep dive into the stories and sounds that shaped the city, followed by time to explore a creative hub known for its industrial charm and local makers. Enjoy a relaxed afternoon of wine and whiskey tasting before wrapping up the day with a Nashville-famous dinner that's bold, flavorful, and well worth the hype.

Start

Elliston Place Soda Shop

2105 Elliston Pl.
Nashville, TN 37203

Elliston Place Soda Shop is a classic, old-school diner that feels like stepping back in time. Known for its made-to-order breakfast, thick hand-spun milkshakes, and nostalgic charm, this longtime Nashville favorite has been serving locals for decades. Every table is outfitted with its own jukebox, setting the scene for a relaxed, retro start to your day.

It's the kind of place where comfort food, conversation, and a little bit of nostalgia come together perfectly. An ideal first stop for your date ahead!

Second Stop

Bicentennial Capitol Mall State Park

600 James Robertson Pkwy.
Nashville, TN 37243

Bicentennial Capitol Mall State Park is a must-visit stop that blends history, open space, and some of the best views in the city. If you arrive at the top of the hour, stand beneath the Carillon columns, positioning yourself in the open space between the pillars. From here, you can listen as music plays from the carillon above, creating a surprisingly peaceful and memorable moment.

As you explore the park, you'll also be treated to incredible views of the Tennessee State Capitol rising at the north end of the mall. It is the perfect place to slow down, take in the surroundings, and soak up a little Nashville history before continuing your date.

Third Stop
Nashville Farmers Market
900 Rosa L Parks Blvd.
Nashville, TN 37208

No matter the time of year, there is always something to see, do, and eat at the Nashville Farmers' Market. This lively spot is filled with indoor vendors offering everything from local goods to international flavors, making it an easy place to wander and explore at your own pace.

Depending on the day, you may find food trucks parked outside, outdoor vendors selling handmade products, and a greenery and nursery area that adds a fresh, seasonal touch. Whether you're grabbing a quick bite, browsing, or just taking it all in, the Farmers' Market is one of those places where it is easy to linger a little longer.

Fourth Stop
Musicians Hall of Fame and Museum
401 Gay St.
Nashville, TN 37219

The Musicians Hall of Fame is a celebration of the artists who shaped the sound of music across every genre. Unlike museums that focus on performers alone, this space honors the musicians, producers, and industry professionals who worked behind the scenes to create the songs we all know and love.

Inside, you'll find immersive exhibits, legendary instruments, and stories that bring music history to life. Whether you're a lifelong music fan or simply curious, this stop offers a deeper appreciation for the talent and teamwork that helped define Music City.

Fifth Stop

Marathon Motor Works

1305 Clinton St STE 100

Nashville, TN 37203

Marathon Motor Works is a fun and lively spot that has something for everyone. Start by tasting wines at our favorite, Grinders Switch. Such a fun spot with great employees and delicious cheese pairing options.

You can also grab free samples of amazing whiskey at Tennessee Legend Distillery, browse the shops for local goods and souvenirs, and take your time exploring the collection of historic cars and old factory equipment.

While walking around inside, you can easily find plaques with fascinating history about the cars, equipment, and the building, making it easy to spend a little extra time. It's the perfect mix of tasting, shopping, and exploring all in one unique Nashville spot.

Final Stop

Hattie B's Hot Chicken

112 19th Ave S.

Nashville, TN 37203

No day in Nashville would be complete without a stop at Hattie B's, a city favorite known for its legendary hot chicken. The perfectly crispy, flavorful chicken comes in a range of heat levels, so you can choose your own adventure from mild to "spicy enough to make you sweat." Hot chicken salads and sandwiches add even more variety. Pair your meal with classic Southern sides and a refreshing drink, and you've got a dinner that's as fun as it is delicious. The casual, lively atmosphere makes it the perfect spot to end your day with big flavors and a little Nashville charm.

Add Your Photos

Keepsakes

Thank you for joining us on this mystery city-date adventure! We hope you've enjoyed the delightful experiences and memorable moments we've crafted just for you in Nashville's North End.

But the adventure doesn't stop here. Keep discovering exciting mystery dates in other cities and uncover new experiences across the U.S. by visiting DatesintheStates.com. There, you can find both physical copies and digital downloads of our mystery date books.

We'd love to see your adventure! Tag us in your date photos on social media @datesinthestates.

About the Creators

Crystal, the writer and creator, is a storyteller at heart. When she's not uncovering hidden gems for the next date night idea, she runs her own digital marketing company, helping small businesses improve their content marketing, increase visibility in their communities, and streamline their online presence.
Visit: crystalstatskey.com

Shane, her husband and partner in adventure, is a dedicated personal trainer and the owner of Beekstar Fitness in Irondequoit, NY. He specializes in working with clients who have limited mobility, helping them build muscle and focus on pain areas so they can regain strength and confidence in their daily lives.
Visit: beekstarfitness.com

Crystal and Shane have explored every U.S. state except Alaska (coming soon!) and are now visiting countries in alphabetical order. Whether road-tripping or curating Mystery Date experiences, they're always chasing their next adventure.

Local Love

A few local gems in North Nashville worth exploring on your next date.

CLIMB NASHVILLE WEST
ROCK CLIMBING GYM
3600 CHARLOTTE AVE, NASHVILLE, TN 37209

ADELE'S
AMAZING WEEKEND BRUNCH
1210 MCGAVOCK ST, NASHVILLE, TN 37203

HUSK
SOUTHERN MEALS IN A HISTORIC MANSION
37 RUTLEDGE ST, NASHVILLE, TN 37210

Want to see your business here? See the next page for details on how to join!

Want to be featured?

MYSTERY DATE BOOK PACKAGES

—

Are you a small business looking to reach new customers? Feature your business in our next Mystery Date Book! Choose from our partnership packages below to connect with couples seeking unique experiences and exclusive deals.

Package One
LOCAL LOVE LISTING
—

A quick shoutout to show you're part of the neighborhood vibe.

Listed in the "Local Love" section of your designated neighborhood date book

Includes business name, address, and social link

Optional: Offer a small promo (e.g., 10% off for book holders)

1 social media shout-out when the book launches

Package Two
FEATURE STOP
—

You're not just a business— you're part of the experience.

Marked as a "Must-Stop" on a Mystery Date

Full-page feature in the book with your story, offerings and photo

Includes 1 social media feature — a dedicated post and story highlighting your business

Note: To ensure each feature is genuine and experience-based, we require a hosted visit prior to inclusion.

Package Three
PARTNER & SELLER
—

Be the spot and the source.

Everything in Tier 2

PLUS: Option to sell the Mystery Date Books at your location

Includes a bulk purchase of 10 books (yours to price + sell)

Keep 100% of the profits from in-store sales

Bonus: Have a featured "sponsored by" page and listed as an official pickup location in our promotions

Prices are subject to change

Feel free to reach us at any time by sending us an email to say hi and to learn more! We look forward to hearing from you.

| www.datesinthestates.com | datesinthestatesblog@gmail.com |

Sponsors & Affiliates

Our sponsors and affiliates help make our adventures possible! Explore the amazing brands and businesses that support our community.

Wanderful

Wanderful is a global community for women who love to travel. Connect, explore, and join a local hub near you!

US Ghost Adventures

Take a ghost tour in one of many major US cities! Save 10% off with code: DATES10

HomeExchange

HomeExchange lets you swap homes with travelers worldwide for authentic, affordable stays. Join today and travel differently!

Loved this date? Keep the adventure going!

You can find Mystery City Date Books at select local stores near you, or visit our website for the most up-to-date list of places to purchase.

Prefer to shop online? Our online shop is open at DatesintheStates.com. You can also find our books on AbeBooks.com and Walmart.com
Just search "Mystery Date Book."

DATES IN THE STATES

A COUPLE TRAVELING THE UNITED
STATES ON A BUDGET

🌐

datesinthestates.com

✉

datesinthestatesblog@gmail.com

📍

Based in Rochester, NY

CONNECT WITH US ON SOCIAL!
@DATESINTHESTATES